MY FIRST GUIDE to WEATHER

MY
FIRST
GUIDE
to
WEATHER

Camilla
de la Bedoyere

Cinyee
Chiu

BPP

CONTENTS

What Is Weather?

Changing Weather

BIRD HUNT

Can you find the peregrine falcons hiding in this book? There is one in every scene except one.

Go to page 57 to find out which scene is the exception.

World Weather

Extreme Weather

Cumulonimbus cloud

Snowflakes

What Is Weather?

Lightning

Rain

Hail

Cirrus clouds

Sunshine

Wind

Icicles

Frost

Fog

UP IN THE AIR

Our planet is wrapped in a blanket of air called the atmosphere. This is where our weather is made. Weather is changing all the time, all over the world.

The atmosphere is made up of air. There are invisible gases in air, such as carbon dioxide, water vapor, and oxygen.

The bottom layer of the atmosphere is called the troposphere. The air in this layer is always moving around. It swirls, whirls, and flows through the sky, turning the weather warm, wet, or windy.

On a fine summer's day, flowers open their petals to take in the sun's warm rays.

Rain clouds drop cooling showers that dampen the ground below.

Whistling winds can blow through trees and meadows, making leaves dance and seeds fly.

Above the troposphere, the atmosphere is thinner the higher up you go.

Warm air inside a hot-air balloon lifts it up into the sky.

Moving air is called wind. The wind blows warm and cold air around the planet, bringing new weather.

Wind turbine

Solar panels

The atmosphere makes the world a good place for life. It helps keep our planet just the right temperature—not too hot and not too cold. It is also full of the gases people, animals, and plants need to survive.

THE SUN

The world's weather starts with the sun. Our sun is a star—a huge ball of glowing gas in space. It gives off energy that bathes our planet in heat and light.

The sun is very big and very old! If the sun were the size of a front door, the Earth would be the size of a coin. It is 4.5 billion years old!

A ray of sunlight takes about 8 minutes and 20 seconds to reach the Earth.

The sun is a long way away. It's about 400 times farther away from the Earth than the moon is. Yet we can feel the energy from the sun as heat and we can see it as sunlight.

Sunlight enables our bodies to make vitamin D, which helps keep us healthy.

①
The sun rises in the east, marking the start of a new day.

Sunlight is made up of different colors of light. As sunlight passes through the air, the blue light is scattered more than the other colors. That's why we see the sky as blue.

Blue light

2

At midday, the sun is high in the sky, right above us. Its energy and light are reaching us directly rather than at an angle.

The sun warms the Earth, and the atmosphere traps the Earth's heat close to it. This keeps our planet warm. The warmed air in the atmosphere has energy, and that makes it move around, helping to create weather.

The sun's energy can burn us, so it's a good idea to protect your skin by covering up or using sunscreen.

Plants need sunlight to grow. They use the sun's energy to make food from water and air. Many animals eat plants, and so the sun's energy is passed on to other living things on Earth.

3

In the evening, the sun sinks below the horizon in the west.

5

THE WIND

Wind is air that is moving from one place to another. Powerful winds blow all over the world. Even though we cannot see the wind, we can see how it moves things and we can feel it on our skin.

③ Water in the warm air may form clouds.

The wind blows in places with both warm air and cold air. The difference in temperature makes the air move.

② Warm air is lighter than cool air, so it rises.

④ Cold air sinks below the warm, rising air. This movement of air is wind.

① The sun warms the ground.

A gentle breeze makes leaves flutter, but when strong winds blow, trees can fall over. The speed of the wind can be measured using the Beaufort scale, which goes from 0 (no wind) to 12 (hurricane). Here are some of the other Beaufort scale levels:

2 | LIGHT BREEZE
Grasses and flowers on long stems sway a little in the wind. Leaves rustle.

3 | GENTLE BREEZE
Leaves and small twigs on trees are moving constantly.

Some winds circle the Earth. Jet streams are strong winds that flow high up in the atmosphere, from west to east. There are four jet streams that blow around the Earth and affect the weather.

Polar jet streams flow in the Northern Hemisphere and the Southern Hemisphere.

North Pole

The area around the equator gets the most light and heat from the sun, so the air there is warm.

Equator

Subtropical jet streams flow above and below the equator.

The North and South Poles don't get much sun, so the air there tends to be cool or cold.

South Pole

4 MODERATE BREEZE
Leaves, small branches, and clothes on a clothesline are lifted.

5 FRESH BREEZE
Small trees sway, and kites are lifted.

6 STRONG BREEZE
It is difficult to hold an umbrella when strong breezes blow. Even large branches in the trees sway!

As wind whips across the top of the ocean, it makes waves. The frothy tops of cresting waves are called whitecaps.

7

WATER

We can't always see it, but water is all around us. Water is always on the move in the air, on land, and in the oceans. The way that water moves around the planet is called the water cycle.

① When the sun heats water, it turns into water vapor (an invisible gas). Plants make water vapor, too. They soak up water from the ground, and water vapor escapes from their leaves into the atmosphere.

② High up, water vapor cools and forms tiny water droplets. This is called condensation. These droplets form clouds.

Water vapor from plants rises in the air.

Water vapor from the ocean rises in the air.

③ Clouds grow bigger as more and more water vapor condenses into tiny droplets. Moving air high up in the sky blows clouds to different places.

④ When enough droplets combine in a cloud that they become too heavy to float in the sky any longer, they fall as rain. If the air is very cold, the clouds are made of ice crystals instead of water droplets. Ice crystals can fall as snow.

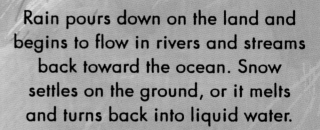

⑤ Rain pours down on the land and begins to flow in rivers and streams back toward the ocean. Snow settles on the ground, or it melts and turns back into liquid water.

⑥ Some of the rainwater stays in lakes. Water also soaks into the ground and porous rocks. There it is called groundwater.

CLOUDS

Clouds sail across the sky like ships on the ocean. As they move, clouds grow bigger or shrink. They can also change their shape and color.

Clouds are not just rain makers. Their size, shape, and color can tell us about the weather that is on its way.

There are three main types of clouds: Puffy clouds are called cumulus clouds. Clouds that grow in long, flat layers are called stratus clouds. Wispy, feathery clouds are called cirrus clouds.

Cumulonimbus cloud

A cumulus cloud grows upward in puffs and is sometimes called a cauliflower cloud.

Stratus cloud

CUMULUS CLOUDS

Cumulus (KYOO-myuh-lus) clouds are fluffy and puffy. They often appear in a blue sky on a warm, sunny day. If they grow, they can turn into towering thunderclouds called cumulonimbus (KYOO-myuh-loh-NIM-bus) clouds.

STRATUS CLOUDS

Stratus clouds stretch across the sky like gray blankets. They grow low in the sky. When they fill the sky, we say the sky is overcast.

CIRRUS CLOUDS

Cirrus clouds form high up in the sky where it is so cold that the water vapor freezes into tiny crystals of ice. Cirrus clouds are often seen in a blue sky, but they can indicate that rain or snow is on its way.

Cirrus clouds

Mares' tails

MARES' TAILS

When strong winds blow through a cirrus cloud, they can shape the ice crystals into long, icy streaks that are called mares' tails.

Mackerel sky

ALTOCUMULUS CLOUDS

A sky that is dotted with high white clouds that look like fish scales is called a mackerel sky. The clouds are altocumulus clouds, and this pattern means that a change in the weather is coming.

Clouds appear when enough water vapor in the air and the air is cooled and forms water droplets.

Clouds disappear when they warm up. The droplets of water inside a cloud turn back into invisible water vapor.

Nimbostratus cloud

NIMBOSTRATUS CLOUDS

Nimbostratus clouds are so dark they can block out the sunlight. They can bring heavy rainfall that goes on for hours, or even a snowstorm.

SNOW AND ICE

Brrr! It's getting chilly, and water is turning to ice. Fluffy flakes of snow slowly fall from low gray skies, and ice crystals sparkle.

Frozen water can fall as snowflakes. It can also fall as hard lumps of ice called hail. If the ice melts slightly as it falls, it forms a mixture of ice and rain called sleet.

Ice crystal

Snowflakes are clusters of ice crystals. Every ice crystal has six sides, or arms, and a different pattern from all the others. Snowflakes form in the atmosphere when ice crystals grow bigger or clump together. Once they are heavy enough to fall, the flakes begin their journey to the ground.

A heavy snowstorm is called a blizzard. Sometimes so much snow falls that it is difficult to see much farther than your fingertips! This is called a whiteout.

Snow can collect in thick piles called snowdrifts, especially around buildings.

When snow melts, it turns back into liquid water and drips from surfaces such as trees, cliffs, and roofs. If those drips freeze again, they make icicles that hang down like pointed teeth.

Icicle

Water on the ground and in ponds freezes into sheets of slippery ice.

A thin blanket of ice crystals sometimes covers the ground and plants. This is called frost, and it often appears after a chilly cloudless night. Frost crystals grow from water vapor in the air, just like snow crystals, but they form on the ground or other surfaces rather than in clouds.

Frost turns cobwebs into sparkly spirals.

Weather satellite

Swallows

Wind sock

Seaweed

Changing Weather

Barometer

Thermometer

Morning glory
flowers

Weather vane

Rain gauge

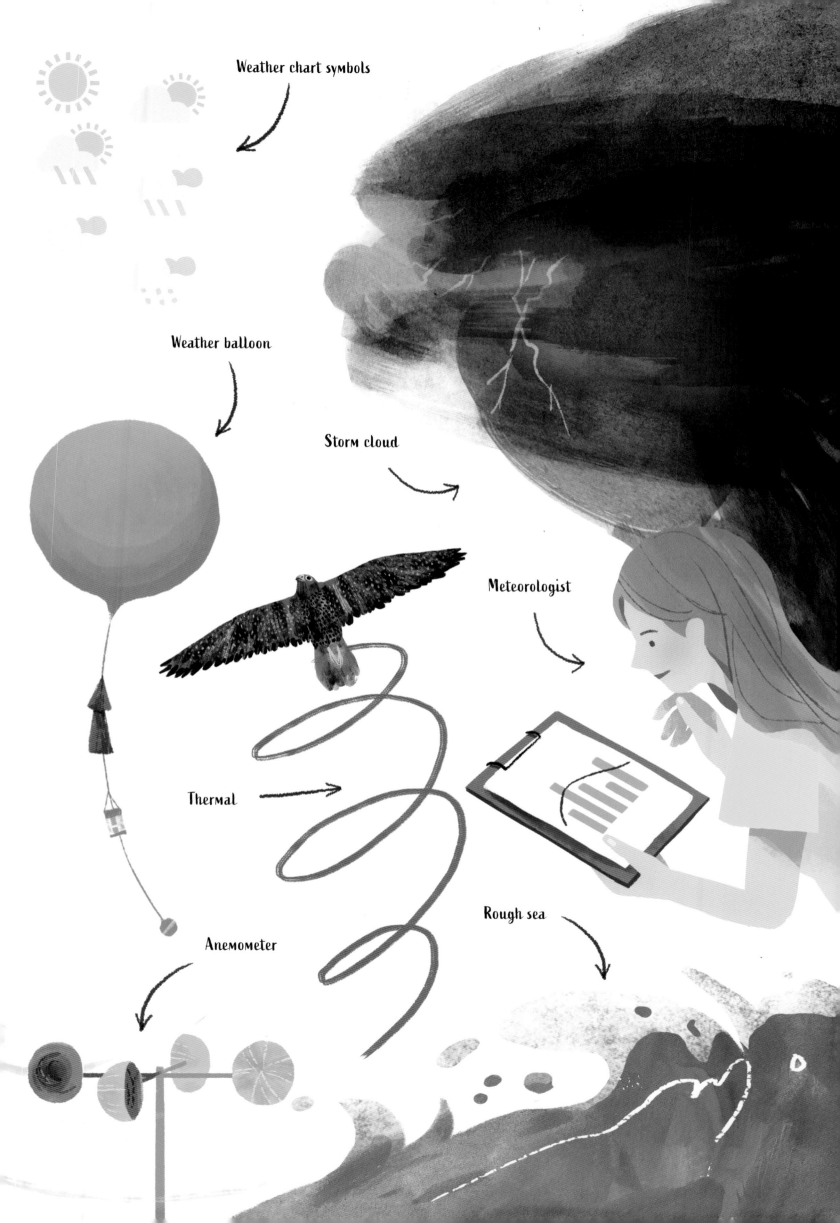

Weather chart symbols

Weather balloon

Storm cloud

Meteorologist

Thermal

Rough sea

Anemometer

LAND AND SEA

Land and sea affect the weather. Follow this falcon on her journey as she soars and swoops all the way from a mountain to seaside cliffs. She will see different types of weather along the way.

A spiral of rising warm air is called a thermal.

The weather on a mountaintop can be harsh. Strong winds howl and sweep across the peak, which is cloaked in cold clouds and mist. Some mountaintops are covered in snow all year. Snow reflects the sun and can be very bright.

Tall mountains make warm winds rise higher.

The falcon joins the thermal and lets the warm, swirling air carry her up high. It's much easier to fly this way.

2

As she flies over a city, the falcon sees plenty of tall buildings. She can spy other falcons nesting in them!

The temperature in a city is higher than in green spaces around it, especially at night. On a sunny day, buildings warm up and stay hot for longer than fields, parks, or woodlands.

Air pollution is made of particles that come from vehicles, factories, and fires.

It rains more by the ocean than it does inland. Warm, wet winds blow across the water and onto land. They can bring rain and fog.

Nest

Sea breezes blow onto land during the day. At night, a land breeze blows onto the ocean.

3

The falcon has reached a cliff by the ocean. Her mate is waiting for her there. He has been taking care of the chicks in the nest.

NATURE'S WEATHER WARNINGS

Look closely at nature and you can see signs that the weather may be about to change. Even tiny differences in the air and temperature can affect how animals and plants behave.

On a damp day, a pine cone stays closed, keeping its seeds safe and dry.

On a dry day, a pine cone is open, and the wind may carry away some of its seeds.

PINE CONES DEPEND ON THE WEATHER TO CARRY THEIR SEEDS

There are tiny seeds inside a pine cone. They need the wind to lift them out of the pine cone and carry them to a place where they can grow into new trees.

RED SKY AT MORNING, SAILORS TAKE WARNING. RED SKY AT NIGHT, SAILORS DELIGHT.

This old saying is true in some parts of the world. It means that if there is a red evening sky, the weather will probably be fine the next day, but if the morning sky is red, then storms may be coming.

Crickets chirp by rubbing their legs against their wings.

CRICKETS CHIRP ON HOT DAYS

Crickets chirp to talk to one another. When the insects are warm, their chirps are faster and louder. On a hot, steamy day, their noisy songs warn that a thunderstorm may be on its way.

WHEN SWALLOWS FLY HIGH, THE WEATHER IS DRY

Swallows often fly high on a warm, dry day. They are chasing the flying insects that have been swept up by warm currents of air.

Swallows swoop and dive to pluck insects from the air.

SEAWEED SWELLS WHEN IT IS WET AND SHRIVELS UP IN FINE, DRY WEATHER

Seaweed grows in the ocean, especially along the coast. People who live by the sea sometimes hang it outside their houses and use it to predict the weather.

Morning glory with open flowers

SOME FLOWERS PROTECT THEMSELVES FROM RAIN BY CLOSING THEIR PETALS

Scarlet pimpernels and morning glory plants open their flowers up to the sun and buzzing bees on fine, warm days. They close their flowers when the weather is turning wet.

Morning glory with closed flowers

A STORM IS COMING

Thunderclouds grow tall and turn dark when they are full of water and ready to burst. Soon, there will be flashes of lightning zipping through the sky and loud rumbles of thunder.

After a long spell of hot weather, small cumulus clouds join together and begin to grow into one bigger cloud. A storm is on the way . . .

Cumulonimbus cloud

Cumulus cloud

③ Inside the cloud, air, water, and ice swirl around. The cloud becomes full of energy and power.

② The cloud grows even taller, towering high into the sky. It is now a thundercloud, or cumulonimbus cloud.

① The hot ground heats the air above it. The hot air rises into the cloud.

The bottom of the cumulonimbus cloud is dark and flat.

The top of a cumulonimbus cloud can be 7½ miles/12 kilometers high—that's 37 times taller than the Eiffel Tower!

④ THIS THUNDERCLOUD IS ABOUT TO BURST!
Droplets of water in the cloud grow bigger. When they get too heavy, they begin to fall as rain. Sometimes heavy ice crystals grow and fall as hailstones.

⑦ The heavy rainfall cools the ground and stops it from warming the air above. The cloud will soon disappear.

As the air rises, the water vapor condenses into water droplets.

UPDRAFT

Warm upward flows of air are called updrafts.

⑤ As ice crystals rub against each other, they make electricity. A bolt of lightning zips through the sky.

DOWNDRAFT

As air cools, it falls in a downdraft.

⑥ Lightning is much hotter than the surface of the sun! The heat makes the air expand, and this creates a mighty noise called thunder.

Lightning zigzags between the cloud and the ground.

The light from lightning travels faster than the sound of thunder. You can tell how far away a storm is by how many seconds pass between the flash and the rumble. Five seconds means the storm is a mile away.

WEATHER FORECASTS

We can measure the weather. Keeping a record of the hours of sunlight, the amount of rain, and the direction of wind helps us work out how the weather is changing. This is called weather forecasting.

A wind gauge is called an anemometer. It measures the speed of the wind. A weather vane shows the direction the wind is blowing.

Anemometer

Weather vane

Thermometer

A barometer is used to measure air pressure, which is the force of air pressing down on the ground. Air pressure is useful in working out how the weather will change.

Barometer

A thermometer measures temperature. We use it to find out how hot or cold the air is. As the air gets hotter, the temperature rises. As the air cools, the temperature gets lower.

When air pressure is high, the weather is likely to be clear and settled. When air pressure is low, the weather is likely to turn cloudy and wet.

A rain gauge is a simple way to record how much rain has fallen. We can keep records over a long time to see how rainfall changes over a year or over many years.

Over time, the temperature and rainfall can be recorded on a graph.

Rain gauge

To help measure the weather, many observations can be made by **weather balloons and satellites** in space.

Weather satellite

Weather satellites travel in space above the atmosphere. They can take photographs of clouds and weather events such as storms. They can also measure the temperature of ocean water and even measure the air moving in the clouds.

A weather balloon is filled with a gas that makes it float upward.

It can rise 20 miles/32 kilometers. The highest a weather balloon has ever flown is 32 miles/ 51 kilometers.

Eventually, the balloon pops!

A weather balloon measures the weather high up in the atmosphere. It carries equipment that can measure air pressure, wind, and temperature. It sends the data back to Earth using satellites.

Computers collect observations from all over the world. They use all this information to forecast the weather.

WEATHER CHARTS

Weather maps, or charts, show what the weather is now or what it will be in the days or weeks ahead. The first weather charts were drawn by hand. Today, computers are used instead.

Once weather and climate data have been collected, they can be used to make a chart like this one. Symbols are used for different types of weather, such as rain and wind.

77°F / 25°C

FRONTS

The wind moves large masses of air around the world. The places where different air masses meet are called fronts, and they bring a change in weather.

WARM FRONT

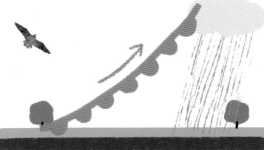

A warm front forms where a mass of warm air is pushing slowly into a mass of cooler air. It may cause rain clouds to form.

COLD FRONT

A cold front happens when cold air quickly pushes warm air up and away. Cold fronts make storm clouds and rain.

15

68°F / 20°C

SYMBOLS

A weather chart uses signs and symbols on a map to show what type of weather is occurring or expected in different places.

TEMPERATURE

The temperature is shown as a number. If the number is blue, then the temperature is at or below 32°F /0°C, which is the freezing point of water.

41°F / 5°C   28°F / −2°C

66°F / 19°C

A warm front is shown as a red line with semicircles pointing in the direction it is moving.

72°F / 22°C

A cold front is shown as a blue line with triangles pointing in the direction it is moving.

68°F / 20°C

63°F / 17°C

WIND

The direction of wind is often shown by an arrow. A number with the arrow shows how fast the wind is blowing.

The study of weather is called meteorology, and the scientists who study it are called meteorologists. They make forecasts using the information that has been collected by satellites and calculated by computers.

Weather charts are a useful way to show how and why meteorologists think the weather will change. The weather can change quickly, so charts are always being updated.

WEATHER RECORDS

Extreme weather and unusual weather events have set world records. These events are rare, but as our climate changes, many of these records are being broken.

DEATH VALLEY, USA

The temperature in the USA's hottest and driest desert has reached a scorching 130°F/54.4°C! It is hard for animals and plants to survive in such extreme heat. Even prickly cacti struggle to live in places where rocks are hot enough to fry eggs.

ATACAMA DESERT, CHILE

Parts of the Atacama Desert can go for years without a drop of rain. That makes it the driest place on Earth. When it does rain, pink flowers spring to life and cover the ground.

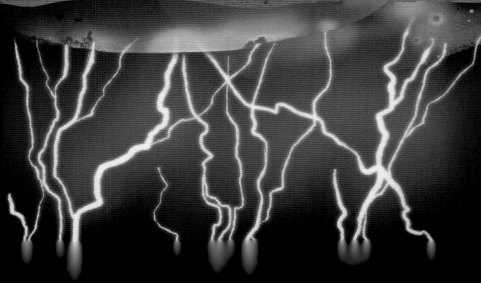

LAKE MARACAIBO, VENEZUELA

This lake in South America is the perfect place to watch lightning strikes. Warm air rises over the lake and clashes with cold winds that come from nearby mountains. There are about 300 thunderstorms every year. Thousands of flashes of lightning zip through the night sky

GIANT HAILSTONES

Giant hailstones are rare, and it is hard to measure them because they start to melt as soon as they crash to the ground. The largest ones on record are more than 8 inches/20 centimeters in diameter.

ANTARCTICA

Antarctica is the world's coldest place. In some parts of this ice-covered land, the temperature never rises above freezing. The world's coldest temperature of −128.6°F/ −89.2°C was recorded here. The weather is far too cold for plants and most animals, although scientists do stay there.

WASHINGTON STATE, USA

The mountains here are some of the world's snowiest places. In just one winter, nearly 93 feet/ 28 meters of snow fell. That's enough to bury a tall building!

MAWSYNRAM AND SOHRA, INDIA

The people who live in these two towns in Northeast India are used to rain. Almost 40 feet/12 meters can fall in a year, and in 1861, around 86 feet/ 26 meters of rain fell in Sohra.

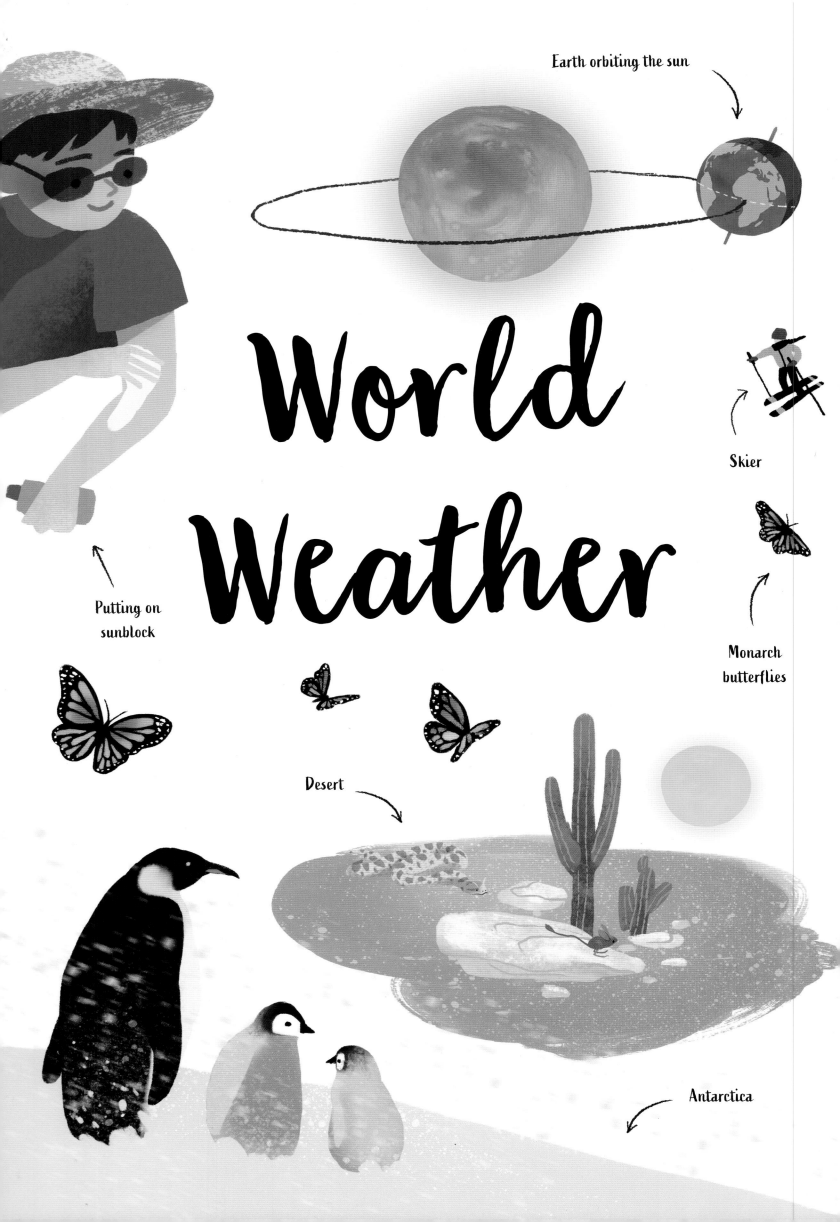

Earth orbiting the sun

World Weather

Skier

Putting on sunblock

Monarch butterflies

Desert

Antarctica

Hang glider

Arctic terns

Winter
tree

Fall
tree

Summer tree

Fox cub

Spring
tree

Farmer in a
temperate region

Farmer in a
tropical region

Bananas

WARM EARTH

In the past, the Earth's climate has often been much warmer than it is today, with no ice anywhere.

Earth explodes with life during hotter periods. In a hot, wet climate, lots of plants grow, and that means there is plenty of food for animals. During a warm period, there are more animals and plants than during a cold period.

This is how the Earth looked during the Late Jurassic, which lasted from 163 million to 145 million years ago. It was part of a long warm period. There were vast forests with conifer trees and huge ferns, but no flowers. Dinosaurs roamed the land, flying reptiles called pterosaurs swooped in the sky, and big swimming reptiles grew more than 20 feet/6 meters long.

Flying reptiles called pterosaurs flapped their wings or glided on the warm winds.

Pliosaurs resembled crocodiles but had flippers instead of feet.

Cycads appeared before the dinosaurs, and they still live in warm places today.

Trees grew tall in the warm climate, but long-necked dinosaurs like the diplodocus could still reach their leaves. This mighty dinosaur measured more than 100 feet/ 30 meters from its nose to the tip of its tail.

Seed

Diplodocus

Most plants today grow their seeds in flowers and fruits, but in the Jurassic period, few plants grew this way. Most plants needed the wind to carry their pollen to other plants. The wind also carried their seeds to new places where they could grow.

Stegosaurus

The allosaurus was a large, meat-eating dinosaur.

The first birds, such as the archaeopteryx, looked like feathery, flying dinosaurs.

The dinosaurs and pterosaurs died out 66 million years ago. This is believed to have happened because a huge asteroid hit the Earth. Dust blocked out sunlight, and the weather turned cold. Plants died and many animals became extinct.

FROZEN EARTH

In the past, the Earth's climate has sometimes been much colder than it is today, with large sheets of ice across the far north and far south of the planet.

When large parts of the Earth are covered in ice and snow, it is called an ice age. During the last ice age, ice covered most of North America, northern Europe, and Asia. In warmer places, there was very little rain, so deserts formed there.

Woolly mammoths

Woolly rhinos

Big animals were suited to the extreme cold. Woolly mammoths and woolly rhinos had bulky bodies, fur, and a thick layer of fat to keep them warm. These animals could go without food for a long time.

Plants need warmth, water, and sunlight to survive. During the long periods of cold weather, water froze and huge areas of ground were covered in snow. Fewer plants means less food for animals.

THE LAST ICE AGE
The last ice age began about 2.5 million years ago. Ice covered large areas.

TODAY
We are actually in a warmer period of the last ice age. The Earth still has ice caps.

SNOWBALL EARTH
If the whole planet becomes totally covered in ice, it is known as Snowball Earth.

A cave lion's pale fur helped it to hide in the snow while it hunted.

Woolly mammoth calf

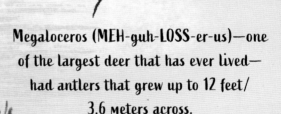

Megaloceros (MEH-guh-LOSS-er-us)—one of the largest deer that has ever lived—had antlers that grew up to 12 feet/ 3.6 meters across.

Beginning about 50,000 years ago, some early humans lived in the world's cold North. They wore animal furs and used tools to hunt. They painted pictures of cave lions and mammoths on the walls of their cave homes, where they took shelter from the weather.

CLIMATES AND SEASONS

The Earth is a planet in space that circles the sun over the course of a year. This giant journey affects the weather in different parts of the world over that time.

(1) As the Earth circles, or orbits, the sun, it also spins. It spins at a tilt around an imaginary line called its axis. This tilt is what gives us seasons.

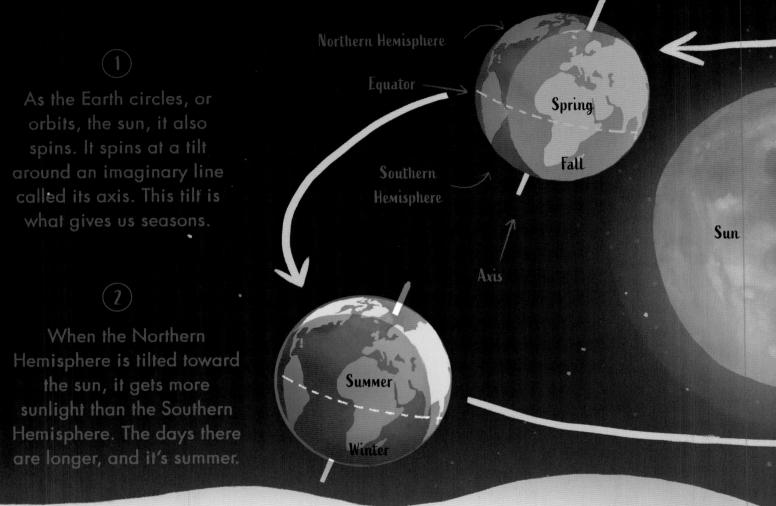

Northern Hemisphere

Equator

Spring

Southern Hemisphere

Fall

Axis

Sun

Summer

Winter

(2) When the Northern Hemisphere is tilted toward the sun, it gets more sunlight than the Southern Hemisphere. The days there are longer, and it's summer.

Areas around the equator are called the tropics. They have a tropical climate, which is hot with plenty of sunshine. Some tropical areas also have wet and dry seasons.

CLIMATES

Climates are patterns of weather that a place experiences over a long period of time.

The areas between the tropics and the polar regions have a temperate climate. The weather there is mild most of the time, and there are four seasons: spring, summer, fall, and winter.

SEASONS

Seasons are parts of a year that have different weather. Seasons happen because the Earth is tilted. When the northern part of the Earth is tilted toward the sun, it is summer in the Northern Hemisphere. Six months later, the southern part of the Earth is tilted toward the sun, so it is summer in the Southern Hemisphere.

④

When the Northern Hemisphere is tilted away from the sun, it gets less sunlight and the days are shorter. It's winter there.

Winter

Summer

When it is winter in the Northern Hemisphere, it is summer in the Southern Hemisphere.

③

In spring and fall, the equator is the closest area to the sun. The days are about the same length in both the Southern and Northern Hemispheres.

Fall

Spring

The polar regions don't get strong sunshine because of the tilt of the Earth. The polar climate is cold, and there are just two seasons: winter and summer. In winter, it is dark even in the daytime, because the sun doesn't rise above the horizon.

During the polar summer, it is light even in the nighttime.

A YEAR OF SEASONS

From spring showers to snowy winters, the weather in temperate woodlands changes with the seasons. The animals and plants change with them.

Trees burst into leaf and blossom.

Birds are busy building nests and laying eggs.

Fruits, seeds, and berries grow and ripen.

Chicks have grown big enough to fly from their nests.

SPRING
The days get longer, and the weather grows warmer. There is plenty of rain, and the wind can be strong and chilly.

Insects buzz around, sipping nectar and collecting pollen.

Many baby animals are born.

Frogs and toads gather in ponds to lay their eggs.

SUMMER
Strong sunshine heats the ground and the air above it. Long, hot days can bring thunderstorms and heavy rains.

Young animals grow strong and begin to explore.

Frogs and newts hide from the hot sun, but snakes and lizards bask.

Insects, such as bees and wasps, look for a dry, safe place to spend the winter.

Some birds and butterflies fly to warmer places for the winter.

Trees with bare branches rest until the spring, when they will burst into life again.

Many trees prepare to survive the winter chill by losing their leaves.

FALL
The nights grow longer, and there is less sunshine to warm the woodland. The weather starts to turn rainy, foggy, or windy.

Mushrooms, which thrive in cool, damp weather, sprout up around tree trunks.

WINTER
The days are short, the weather turns cold, and the skies are often gray and gloomy. Snow, ice, and frost make everything sparkle.

Hungry creatures find the stores of food they hid in the fall.

Animals such as squirrels store food for the winter.

Some animals find snug places to keep warm, where they wait for better weather.

ON THE MOVE

Some animals go on long journeys to avoid winter weather. They set off for places where they can find food or the perfect place to breed.

Arctic terns soar across entire oceans to enjoy a year of endless summers. They are record-breaking travelers, with some flying more than 40,000 miles/ 70,000 kilometers in a year.

JULY TO AUGUST

The terns leave their breeding grounds in Greenland, near the Arctic, before gales cover the land in snow. They fly south across the Atlantic Ocean.

Monarch butterflies migrate by the millions each year to avoid the deadly winter chill. No one is sure how these insects find their way to forests in Mexico and California, but they may use the sun and the Earth's magnetic field.

JULY TO AUGUST

The butterflies feed, mate, and lay their eggs in Canada and the northern United States. Butterflies that emerge from chrysalises in the early fall will soon migrate.

Milkweed plant

Eggs

Caterpillar

Chrysalis

The elephants of Mali, West Africa, live on the edge of one of the world's driest places: the Sahara Desert. They survive the heat and droughts by following the rains. Mali's elephants make the longest migration of any elephants, walking 370 miles/600 kilometers in a year.

NOVEMBER TO MAY

In the dry season, the elephants stay in the north of their range. They find water by traveling between lakes. By May there is almost no water left.

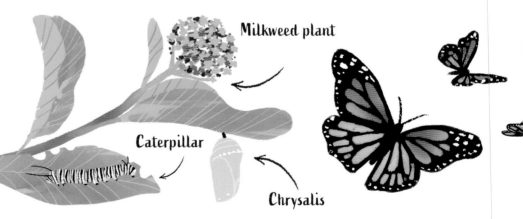

NOVEMBER

After four months, the terns reach the sea around Antarctica. They find plenty of fish to eat before heading north again in April.

MAY TO JUNE

The terns arrive back in Greenland, where they lay their eggs. They raise their chicks in the Northern Hemisphere's summer.

NOVEMBER TO JANUARY

The butterflies fly south to reach cool mountain forests in California and Mexico. They sleep until spring arrives in February, when they start to fly north.

MAY TO JULY

On their journey, the butterflies stop to lay eggs. Each new generation of adults continues the journey north and reaches Canada and the northern United States in the summer.

JUNE TO AUGUST

The elephants listen for thunder and follow the rain clouds. They walk south, where more rain falls at this time of year and plants have grown.

SEPTEMBER TO NOVEMBER

The weather turns dry again. It is time for the elephants to begin migrating back north on their circular route.

PEOPLE AND THE WEATHER

The weather is part of our daily life. Weather can affect what we do, what we eat, how we travel, what clothes we decide to wear, and even how we feel. It can be fun, too!

Light winds and clear skies are the perfect weather conditions for a hot-air balloon ride.

Airplanes fly faster when there is a strong wind behind them.

Wind and atmospheric pressure are useful for flying. Thanks to the weather, there are lots of ways that humans can copy birds, bats, and flying insects by taking to the air.

A parachute allows a person to float safely to the ground.

The sun can burn us, but hats and sunscreen protect our skin.

Wind helps boats to travel. It fills their sails and pushes them across the water.

The wind that whips up the water gives surfers and windsurfers a boost as they ride the waves.

40

It can be difficult to drive cars and buses on snowy roads, but skis slide along easily. Some children who live in cold countries ski to school in winter.

Buses and cars can slip on icy roads, but special snow chains help their tires to grip the smooth surfaces.

Farmers in temperate places grow different foods for each season. Most food crops, including beans, potatoes, and carrots, are harvested in the summer and fall, but some, such as cabbages, can survive the winter.

Farmers in the tropics can pick ripe and juicy fruit from trees all year round. Plants that give us coffee, tea, chocolate, bananas, and pineapples grow only in warm places.

41

Raining frogs

Red rain

Moonbow

Extreme Weather

Tornado

Hurricane-force winds

Sand dunes
and wind

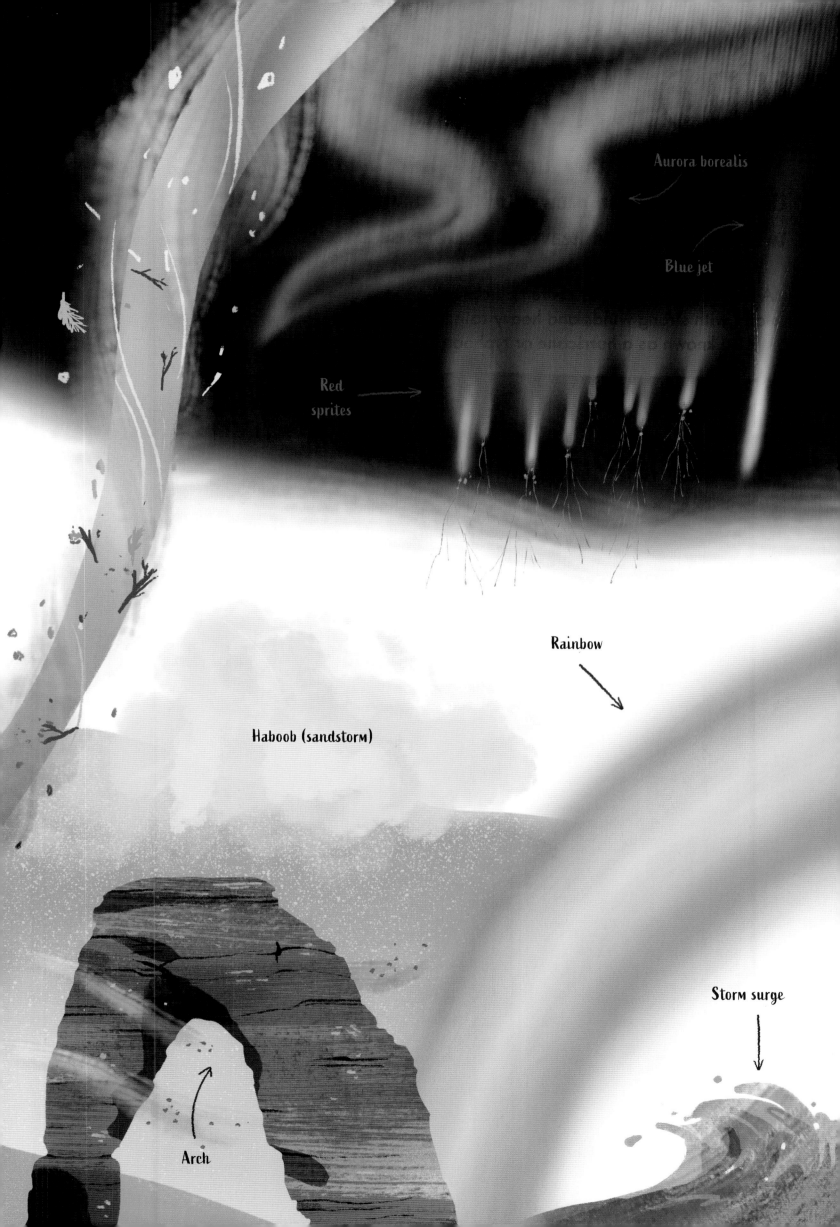

Aurora borealis

Blue jet

Red sprites

Rainbow

Haboob (sandstorm)

Storm surge

Arch

WILD WEATHER

Sometimes the weather turns really wild! When strong winds whirl across the ocean, they can grow into huge, powerful storms. Over land, storms, twisting winds, and heavy rain can cause extreme damage.

A tropical cyclone is an extreme tropical storm with strong winds and heavy rain. It is also known as a hurricane or typhoon.

③ The clouds begin to spiral as strong winds blow.

② The water vapor condenses and forms clouds.

① Warm ocean water evaporates. It turns into water vapor and rises.

The center of the storm is called the eye. The weather there is calm.

Bands of thunderclouds drop heavy rain.

When tropical cyclones move over land, they bring flooding and cause great damage. The wind can be powerful enough to pull trees out of the ground and destroy buildings. However, they soon run out of energy over land.

A tornado is a fast, spinning wind that begins in a thunderstorm. When warmer, moist air meets cool dry air, the whole cloud starts to slowly spin. The winds suck up air, which spirals into a tall funnel. When the funnel touches the ground, a tornado is formed.

A tornado that happens over the sea is called a waterspout.

④ The clouds spread out at the top of the storm like a huge disk.

A tornado moves quickly over the ground.

A cyclone can be hundreds of miles across.

Mudslide

A cyclone can push huge amounts of water onto land. This is called a storm surge.

When heavy rain falls over mountains, it can create a mudslide. The rainwater mixes with the soil to make a thick sludge that flows like water. Mudslides are more likely in places where people have cut down trees or other plants.

45

EXTREME HOT AND COLD

Deserts are very dry places that experience extreme temperatures. These conditions make it difficult for living things to survive, but even in the Sahara and Gobi Deserts, there are signs of life.

Addax

Lappet-faced vulture

In the Sahara, dry winds stir up sandstorms called haboobs.

Barbary sheep

Many deserts have hot climates with strong sunshine and few clouds. The Sahara is the world's largest hot desert. Temperatures can soar above 122°F /50°C but turn cool at night.

Saharan horned viper

Desert animals can cope with hot weather and droughts.

Many plants that live in hot deserts have small leaves that do not lose water easily. Some plants store water in fat leaves or stems.

Gazelle

Ostrich

Rain rarely falls in the Sahara, but in valleys called wadis, water collects and creates oases. Plants grow there, and animals visit to drink.

The Gobi Desert, in Asia, is called a cold desert. During the long winters there, the temperature can drop to −36°F /−38°C. The Gobi Desert is so cold and dry that it can experience both sandstorms and snowstorms in one day!

It rarely rains in winter, but snow sometimes blows in from Siberia and lightly frosts the sandy dunes.

Snow-covered sand dunes

Saxaul tree

Most plants cannot live in freezing temperatures. When water in their leaves turns to ice, it kills them. Some plants that live in cold deserts have small waxy leaves that do not freeze.

Snow leopard

Argali sheep

The animals that live here need to find ways to stay warm and survive with little rainfall.

Jerboas dig burrows where they spend the winter.

Bactrian camels have thick, woolly coats and store fat in their humps.

47

STRANGE WEATHER

The world can surprise us with some unusual and wonderful weather. Many of us have seen a rainbow, but did you know the weather can give us a moonbow, green shimmers, and red sprites?

A moonbow looks like a halo around the moon.

Aurora lights

Near the poles, particles from the sun sometimes hit the atmosphere and create shimmering curtains of light. In the Northern Hemisphere, they are called the northern lights or aurora borealis. In the Southern Hemisphere, they are called the southern lights or aurora australis.

If strong moonlight passes through raindrops, a ghostly moonbow can form.

① Sunlight is white light, but that white light is made up of all the colors of the rainbow.

Rainbows appear in the part of the sky opposite the sun.

Sunlight

Water droplets

Rainbow

② As sunlight hits water droplets in the air, the white light bends and splits into seven colors.

③ The colors always appear in the same order: red, orange, yellow, green, blue, indigo, and violet.

Blue jets are sparks of lightning that shoot up from the top of a thundercloud.

Red sprites are red lightning flashes that flare up toward space. They appear in groups and last less than a second.

Blue jet

Red sprites

Blue jets and red sprites are rare types of lightning that are best seen from space. Scientists are trying to understand what causes them.

It's raining frogs! The winds in a tornado or waterspout can be so strong that they suck up small animals, then drop the creatures back when the winds lose strength. Some people have reported seeing frogs falling from the sky, while others say they have seen showers of worms, squid, or fish!

Have you ever seen red rain? Storm winds can pick up tiny seeds, or spores, from red algae, or seaweed, and carry them up into rain clouds. When the rain falls, it is red.

WEATHER AT WORK

Over thousands of years, the weather can change the world. Wind, rain, and ice turn mountains into towers of balancing boulders and grind stone into sand. This is called weathering.

The weather has created a formation called the Shilin, or Stone Forest, in soft limestone rocks in China's Yunan Province.

FROST SHATTERING

Rainwater can seep into the cracks in rocks and freeze there. As water freezes into ice, it takes up more space than when it was liquid. Over time this weakens the rock by making the cracks bigger, and small pieces may break off.

Frost-shattered rock

ACID RAIN

Rainwater is not pure water. It is slightly acid and can wear down soft rock such as limestone. Over time, the damaged rock can then be shaped into pillars by wind and further rain.

CARVING CAVES

Acid in rainwater or groundwater dissolves limestone underground, creating caves. Dripping water can create unusual rock structures, such as stalactites and stalagmites.

Stalactites hang down

Stalagmites grow up

TRANSPORTED BY WIND

Desert winds blow sand across the land. The sand collects in hills called dunes. Dunes are always on the move, slowly drifting across the desert.

WIND EROSION

Wind can whip around rocks, carrying tiny pieces of grit or ice crystals that wear the rocks away. This is called erosion. Sometimes the rocks end up in amazing shapes such as arches and mushrooms.

This is a natural arch. The hardest rock is left standing, while softer rock has been eroded by the wind.

A hoodoo, or fairy chimney, is a pillar of soft rock with a top stone of harder rock. Hoodoos are common in deserts.

This mushroom rock has been carved by wind. The wind can carry more sand near the ground, so it erodes the lower layers faster.

When stalactites and stalagmites meet each other, they create columns.

CLIMATE CHANGE

The world's climate has changed over millions of years, but now humans are changing it, too. We are making the world warmer, and that has begun to affect the weather and living things everywhere.

The gases emitted by factories, pipelines, and cars are a type of pollution.

When we burn fossil fuels, they make gases, such as carbon dioxide, which go into the atmosphere.

Carbon dioxide moves from the air into the ocean.

Coal, oil, and gas are types of fossil fuels, which are found in the ground or on the ocean floor. For many years, we have been burning them to make energy to cook food, heat our houses, travel, and make things in factories.

Coral reefs grow in warm, clean saltwater, but if the water gets too hot or too polluted, the coral dies.

Climate change has been warming the oceans, which can affect the patterns of rainfall and temperature around the world. Some places have begun to get more rain, while others don't get enough.

Carbon dioxide and other gases in the atmosphere keep heat from escaping into space. The more of these gases there are, the warmer the Earth gets. This changes the weather everywhere.

Heat rises from the warm ground.

Trees are cut down so the land can be used for farming or building. Forests help to keep the climate stable, so losing them affects the weather and can even create deserts.

Buildings and roads stop rainwater from seeping slowly into the ground. This can cause floods.

Many ocean animals, including fish, shellfish, and turtles, may not be able to survive in warmer oceans

A warmer Earth means the ice around the North Pole and South Pole has begun to melt.

ENERGY FOR THE FUTURE

Sunlight, wind, and water can be used to make energy that does not pollute the environment or contribute to climate change. These types of energy are renewable, which means they will not run out. They are good for us and good for the world.

SOLAR POWER

Solar power is a way of collecting energy from sunlight.

Solar panels collect the sun's energy and turn it into electricity. This energy doesn't run out because sunlight is free and there is lots of it!

WIND POWER

The power of the wind can be used to turn special machines called turbines, which make electricity.

A wind farm is a place that has many wind turbines working together. On a windy day, one turbine can make enough electricity for 500 homes.

HYDROPOWER

Flowing water can be used to make electricity. This is called hydropower. At a hydroelectric power station, a high reservoir stores water. The water is held back by a wall called a dam. The water flows through pipes that lead from the reservoir to the turbines below the dam.

When water flows fast through the turbines, they spin and make electricity.

54

There are lots of ways we can use renewable energy, and some are really simple!

We use solar power and wind energy when we dry clothes on a line.

Solar lamp

The sun's energy can be used to power solar lamps or even phone chargers.

Solar charger

Renewable energy can charge batteries, which are then used to power electric vehicles. These vehicles allow us to get around without polluting the air or contributing to climate change.

Electric cars can recharge at special stations.

Some energy companies offer their customers the choice to power their houses with "green energy," meaning energy that comes from renewable sources.

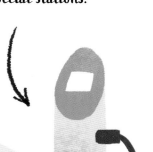

Welcome to Green Power

100% Renewable Energy

Helping to protect the planet for a cleaner future

Electric scooter

WEATHER WORDS

ASTEROID
a piece of rock that falls to Earth from space

ATMOSPHERE
the layer of gases that surrounds the Earth

CARBON DIOXIDE
a type of invisible gas found in the atmosphere

CLIMATE
the pattern of weather that a place experiences over a long time

CONIFER
a type of tree that grows cones and has needle-like or scale-like leaves all year

DESERT
a place that has very little rainfall all year

EQUATOR
an invisible line that divides the Earth into halves

EVAPORATE
to turn from liquid water into water vapor

EXTINCT
describes a species of animal or plant that has died out

HAILSTONES
lumps of ice that sometimes form when rain freezes

HEMISPHERE
one half of the Earth's surface; the equator marks a line between the Northern and Southern Hemispheres

ICE AGE
a long period of time when the Earth's climate cooled down and ice caps formed

BIRD HUNT

You won't spot a falcon on pages 30–31. These birds live almost all over the world today, but they were not alive in the Jurassic.

ICE CAP

a sheet of ice that covers a large area, especially around the North and South Poles

METEOROLOGIST

a person who studies weather and climate

OXYGEN

a type of invisible gas found in the atmosphere; animals depend on it

POLLUTION

something that is damaging to the environment

SEASON

a period of time in a year that has distinctly different weather from other times

TEMPERATE

describes a climate that is mild all year—not very hot and not very cold

TEMPERATURE

a measure of how hot or cold something is

THERMAL

a current of warm air that is moving up

TROPICAL CYCLONE

a strong storm that forms in the tropics; also known as a hurricane

TROPOSPHERE

the lowest layer of the atmosphere

WATER VAPOR

a type of invisible gas found in the atmosphere

WEATHER

the state of the atmosphere, the temperature, and the amount of wind, sunlight, clouds, and rain

FIRST US EDITION 2022
FIRST PUBLISHED BY TEMPLAR BOOKS,
AN IMPRINT OF BONNIER BOOKS UK, 2021

LIBRARY OF CONGRESS CATALOG CARD NUMBER 2021953323
ISBN 978-1-5362-2672-0

22 23 24 25 26 27 LEO 10 9 8 7 6 5 4 3 2 1

PRINTED IN HESHAN, GUANGDONG, CHINA

THIS BOOK WAS TYPESET IN ACTIVE, GARDN CROWN, AND GRAHAM.
THE ILLUSTRATIONS WERE DONE IN WATERCOLOR AND INK
AND FINISHED DIGITALLY.

BIG PICTURE PRESS
AN IMPRINT OF
CANDLEWICK PRESS
99 DOVER STREET
SOMERVILLE, MASSACHUSETTS 02144

WWW.CANDLEWICK.COM

The creators would like to give special thanks to the Royal
Meteorological Society for their valuable contribution to this book.

To find out more about the Royal Meteorological Society,
visit www.rmets.org.